P9-CND-505

Integrity

by Meg Greve

Content Consultants:
Melissa Z. Pierce, L.C.S.W.
Sam Williams, M.Ed.

rourkeeducationalmedia.com

Teacher Notes available at
rem4teachers.com

www.rourkeeducationalmedia.com

Melissa Z. Pierce is a licensed clinical social worker with a background in counseling in the home and school group settings. Melissa is currently a life coach. She brings her experience as a L.C.S.W. and parent to the *Little World Social Skills* collection and the *Social Skills and More* program.

Sam Williams has a master's degree in education. Sam is a former teacher with over ten years of classroom experience. He has been a literacy coach, professional development writer and trainer, and is a published author. He brings his experience in child development and classroom management to this series.

PHOTO CREDITS: Cover: © Christopher Futcher; Page 3: © Chris Bernard; Page 5: © Igor Demchenkov; Page 7: © Lunamarina; Page 9: © Rich Legg; Page 11: © Agnieszka Kirinicjanow; Page 13: © omgimages; Page 15: © Cliff Parnell; Page 17: © Alija; Page 19: © Rhienna Cutler; Page 21: © Catherine Yeulet;

Illustrations by: Anita DuFalla

Edited by: Precious McKenzie

Cover and Interior designed by: Tara Raymo

Library of Congress PCN Data

Integrity / Meg Greve
(Little World Social Skills)
ISBN 978-1-61810-137-2 (hard cover)(alk. paper)
ISBN 978-1-61810-270-6 (soft cover)
Library of Congress Control Number: 2011945282

Rourke Educational Media
Printed in the United States of America,
North Mankato, Minnesota

rourkeeducationalmedia.com

customerservice@rourkeeducationalmedia.com • PO Box 643328 Vero Beach, Florida 32964

Do you always try to do what is right?

If you said yes, then you have **integrity.**

I try to do at least one good deed a day!

Are you **honest** even when no one is looking?

If you find
something that doesn't belong
to you, try to find the owner.
That shows integrity!

If you said yes, then you have integrity.

Acting with integrity is not easy.

Making fun of people is not acting with integrity.

Sometimes you have to be nice
even when you do not want to.

Sometimes you have to say you are **sorry** even when you do not want to.

I try to be a good friend to everyone.

You have integrity if you keep your **promises.**

You have integrity if you **respect** the **feelings** of others.

Taking good care of others shows you have integrity.

Take the Integrity Test!

1. I always try to do what is right. ▢ yes ▢ no

2. I am honest. ▢ yes ▢ no

3. I keep my promises. ▢ yes ▢ no

4. I am a friend to others. ▢ yes ▢ no

5. I respect the feelings of others. ▢ yes ▢ no

If you said yes to all five, then you have integrity!

Picture Glossary

feelings (FEEL-ings):
Emotions you have such as sadness, happiness, jealousy, fear, or anger.

honest (ON-ist):
This is when you are being truthful.

integrity (in-TEG-ruh-tee):
The honest, responsible, and respectable character of a person is called integrity.

promises (PROM-iss-iz):
The things you say you will do no matter what.

respect (ri-SPEKT):
A feeling of thoughtfulness and recognition that something is important.

sorry (SAHR-ee):
Feeling sad or bad about doing something wrong.

Index

Websites

www.charactercounts.org

www.charactersofcharacter.org/games1.html

http://library.thinkquest.org/J001675F/

About the Author

Meg Greve is a teacher, mother, and wife. She always tries to be honest, keep her promises, and act with integrity – even when it's not easy!

Ask The Author!
www.rem4students.com